Birds

Tone Finnanger

David and Charles

A DAVID & CHARLES BOOK

Copyright © J.W. Cappelens Forlag, AS 2010
Cappelen Hobby
www.cappelen.no

First published in the UK in 2010 by David & Charles
Reprinted in 2011, 2013, 2014, 2016, 2017, 2018

David & Charles is an imprint of F&W Media International, Ltd
Pynes Hill Court, Pynes Hill, Exeter, EX2 5AZ

F&W Media International, Ltd is a subsidiary of F+W Media, Inc
10151 Carver Road, Suite #200, Blue Ash, OH 45242, USA

Content and images first published in *Crafting Tilda's Friends, Sew Sunny
Homestyle, Sew Pretty Homestyle, Sew Pretty Christmas Homestyle, Crafting
Springtime Gifts* and *Crafting Christmas Gifts*.

A catalogue record for this book is available from the British Library.

ISBN-13: 978-0-7153-3872-8 hardback
ISBN-10: 0-7153-3872-2 hardback

Printed in China by RR Donnelley
for F&W Media International, Ltd
Pynes Hill Court, Pynes Hill, Exeter, EX2 5AZ

Publisher Ali Myer
Acquisitions Editor Jennifer Fox-Proverbs
Assistant Editor Jeni Hennah
Project Editor Beth Dymond
Design Manager Sarah Clark
Production Controller Bev Richardson
Pre Press Jodie Culpin

F+W Media publish high quality books on a wide range of subjects.
For more great book ideas visit: **www.sewandso.co.uk**

www.ilovetilda.com
For beauty and inspiration in everything Tilda

CONTENTS

Fabrics & Materials.................................6
Stuffed Forms 8

Jolly Geese.................................. 10
Seaside Puffins 16
Floral Doves 20
Royal Hens 24
Duck Pond 28
Bird House 32
Busy Chickens.......................... 36
Oyster Catchers 44

Suppliers.................................... 46
Index.. 46
Templates 47

Fabrics and Materials

Fabrics

Fabrics with a slightly coarse weave are better for making stuffed figures than thin or fine fabrics, as they are much firmer and therefore easier to mould. Linen and plain cotton fabrics are the best types to use, and fabrics with a woven pattern are often preferable to printed patterns. If you would like to use thinner fabrics, you may find it useful to iron a layer of fusible interfacing on the wrong side, to give you a firmer fabric.

When choosing material for the skin colour, use pale linen to create a fair skin tone and light brown linen for darker skin tones. If you are making animals, try using a material with stripes or spots to create an interesting fur effect.

The designs that do not require stuffing, as well as the clothes for the figures and the appliqué projects, can be made from cottons, polyester cottons and most types of fabric. These can therefore be much more decorative than the fabrics used for the stuffed figures.

Fabrics can be bought from craft shops, patchwork and quilting suppliers, and even some department stores. You could also try shops that sell fabrics for curtains and upholstery, which are often a good source for classic patterns and French Toile.

Stuffing

For the projects in this book you will need a good-quality polyester stuffing to fill the figures. A selection of stuffing and wadding can be purchased from most patchwork and quilting shops, as well as from many online retailers.

Fusible interfacing

Fusible interfacing comes in various thicknesses to suit different projects. Volume interfacing is an iron-on fusible wadding (batting) that produces a firm, padded result. Lightweight interfacing is much thinner and is used for stiffening or reinforcing lighter fabrics. Firm interfacing is used for making fabric boxes and large bags, so that the items will stand upright without collapsing. For the best results, choose a fusible interfacing that is slightly lighter in weight than your fabric.

Iron-on adhesive

Bondaweb is a strong double-sided adhesive, which bonds one fabric to another when ironed. The adhesive side is pressed against the reverse side of a material and the paper is torn off, resulting in an adhesive material for simple appliqué work. You can also buy Wonderweb iron-on tape, which is useful for attaching smaller pieces of fabric, such as adding trims.

Accessories

A huge variety of beads, ribbons, buttons and other embellishments can be found in craft shops, or you can collect natural materials to decorate your projects. Tilda products, such as mini gold crowns and dolls' hair, are available from www.pandurohobby.co.uk.

Useful tools

- **A vanishing ink pen**
  Useful for tracing patterns onto fabric. The line disappears when you press it with a damp cloth or after a short while. Alternatively, you can use a fine waterproof fabric pen, or a white gel roller-ball pen for darker fabrics.
- **Small pointed fabric scissors**
  Vital for getting precise shapes when cutting out material.
- **A transparent sewing machine foot**
  Makes it easier to see and follow the pattern that has been traced onto the fabric.
- **A wooden plant stick**
  Useful for turning figures the right way out and inserting stuffing.
- **Craft paints**
  Used for creating faces for the figures and adding details to the clothes and accessories.

Templates

All templates at the back of this book need to be enlarged by 400%. Add seam allowance for all templates, unless otherwise stated.

For details of craft shops and suppliers, please refer to the list on page 46.

Stuffed Forms

Faces

It is always best to wait until any headdresses are in place before you add the face. This makes it easier for you to see where the eyes should be positioned. Insert two pins in the head where the eyes should be. Remove the pins and fix the eyes in the pinholes, using the eye tool from a face kit or the head of a pin dipped in black paint. Blusher or lipstick can be applied with a dry brush to create rosy cheeks.

SEWING

Avoid cutting out the item first unless absolutely necessary. Fold the fabric double, right sides facing, and transfer the pattern to it. Mark any openings for reversing indicated on the pattern. Sew carefully and evenly along the marked lines, using a stitch length of 1.5–2mm (⅛–¾in).

CUTTING OUT

Cut out the item with a narrow seam allowance of 3–4mm (⅛in). Where there are openings for reversing, cut a wider seam allowance of about 7–8 mm (⁵⁄₁₆in). Cut a notch in the seam allowance where the seam curves sharply inwards.

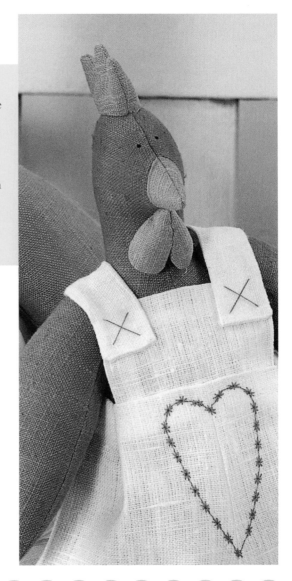

REVERSING

A pointed wooden garden cane or stick is useful for reversing. Use mainly the blunt end, except for details such as the bill on a bird where you can use the sharp end to carefully push it out. To avoid the stick poking through the fabric, trim the tip slightly to make it less sharp.

To reverse long, thin shapes, such as legs and arms, push the blunt end of the stick against the foot, see Figure A. Start close to the foot and pull the leg down along the stick, see Figure B. Continue to pull the leg down the stick until the tip/foot emerges from the opening. Pull the foot while drawing back the bottom so that the leg turns right side out, see Figure C.

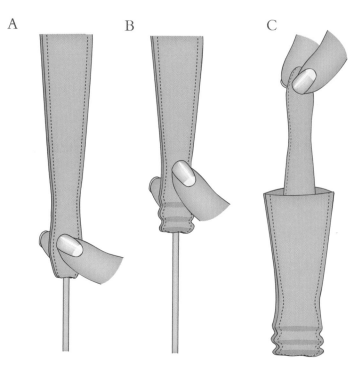

A   B   C

STUFFING

Fold in the extra seam allowance along the opening in the seam. Press the item.

Use your fingers where you can when you are stuffing. Where your fingers won't fit, use the blunt end of a pen or pencil; it will only break through the stuffing and fabric if the tool is too thin.

Push the filling loosely into the item; avoid compressing it into a solid mass before it is in position. Push the filling carefully but firmly into place, adding more filling until you have a firm and well-shaped form. Sew up the opening neatly.

JOLLY GEESE

YOU WILL NEED
- *White or sand-coloured linen for the body and wings*
- *Terracotta linen for the beak, legs and feet*
- *Fabric for clothes*
- *Stuffing*
- *Raffia strips for the bow*
- *Fabric paints for the face*
- *Embroidery threads for the clothes*

HOW TO MAKE

BODY AND WINGS

Read the section on 'Stuffed Forms' on pages 8–9 before starting.

Fold the white linen double, right sides together, and trace the pattern for the body. Cut away enough fabric so that you can sew on two pieces of terracotta linen where the beak will be, and trace the beak. Sew around the body and beak, see Figure A. Cut out, and turn the body inside out.

With the white linen double, trace the pattern for the wings and sew around, see Figure B.

Cut out and turn all the parts inside out. Stuff the body and wings as described on page 9.

A 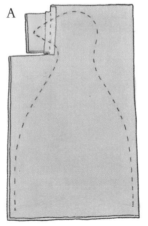   B

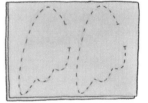

Make bigger geese by enlarging the pattern to 120% on a photocopier.

FEET AND LEGS

Fold the terracotta linen double and trace the feet and leg patterns. Mark extra seam allowances at the bottom of the legs as given on the pattern. Sew around the feet and up the side seams of the legs including the seam allowance, see Figure C. Cut out the pieces and cut a cross opening on each foot as marked on the pattern.

Turn the feet and legs inside out. Fold in the seam allowance at the bottom of the legs before stuffing them. Stuff the feet. Tack the openings of the feet closed and then sew the legs on to the feet so that they conceal the openings, see Figure D.

Insert the legs in to the bottom of the body and sew up the opening fastening the legs. Sew on the wings.

C

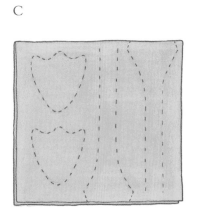

D

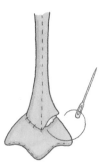

DUNGAREES

Fold the fabric in half and place the pant pattern on the fold. Cut out two dungaree pant pieces, adding extra seam allowances at the waist and the bottom of the legs. Cut out a bib piece with extra seam allowances around three sides.

Place the two pant pieces with right sides together, and sew up one side along the curved edge, see Figure E.

Turn and press the seam allowance across the top and each side of the bib. Insert lengths of iron-on tape and iron to hold.

With right sides facing, sew on the bib across the centre seam of the dungaree pants. Fold down the waist hem and press with the bib up.

Fold the pants with right sides together and sew along the other curved edge.

Fold the dungaree pants the other way so that the seams now match each other and sew the legs, see Figure F.

Press seams open. Fold up the seam allowance at the bottom of each leg, insert iron-on tape and press to hold. Turn inside out and put the dungarees on the figure.

E

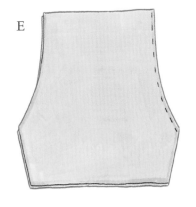

F

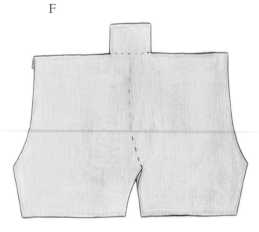

Make two tucks at the front, one on each side of the bib and two at the back so that the dungarees fit at the waist. Stitch the tucks to hold.

To make the straps, fold the fabric in half and place the pattern along the fold. Cut out two straps and sew along the long and one short edge, see Figures G and H. Turn the straps inside out and press.

Put the pants on the figure. Stitch two tucks at the front, one on each side of the bib, and two at the back, so it fits the body. Place the stitched ends of the straps on the front of the bib and attach by hand sewing crosses or adding buttons. Cross them at the back, insert inside the waist and stitch to hold.

Fold a big tuck at the outside bottom edge of each dungaree leg and stitch to hold, see Figure I.

G

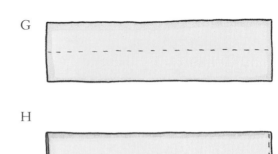

H

I

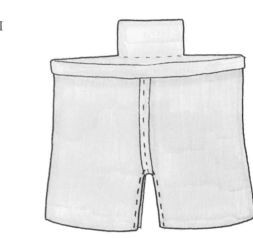

HAT

Fold the fabric for the hat double with right sides together, trace the pattern and sew around it, leaving an opening, see Figure J.

Cut out, turn inside out and press. Fold the half of the hat with the opening into the other half and press, see Figure K.

Embroider around the inner edge of the hat before pressing the brim up at the front and down at the back, see Figure L. Pull the hat firmly on to the head and add a few stitches at the neck and on each side.

Create the face as described on page 8 and tie the raffia strips into a bow around the neck, see Figure M.

J

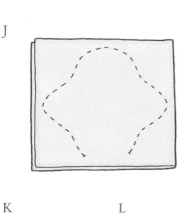

M

K   L

Jolly Geese   15

SEASIDE PUFFINS

HOW TO MAKE

BODY

Read the section on 'Stuffed Forms' on pages 8–9 before starting.

Sew together two pieces of fabric for the upper and lower body. Repeat for the other side. Place together, right sides facing, transfer the pattern and sew around the outline, see Figure A. Cut out, turn right side out and fold in the seam allowance along the opening. Stuff the bird.

A

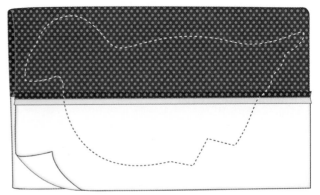

Place the puffins in a pot filled with florist's foam and topped with decorative shells.

Fold the opening so that the seams are aligning. Push and twist the painted wooden canes into the body. Sew up the opening between the sticks, see Figure B.

WINGS
Fold the fabric for the wings and eye patches double, right sides facing. Transfer the patterns, sew around, leaving reversing openings, and cut out. Turn right side out and press. Stuff the wings. Sew up the opening and attach.

B

FINISHING TOUCHES

Attach the eye patches. Sew a row of running stitches around the edge with black embroidery thread (floss). Paint the bill, see Figure C.

Sew three lines for the eyes with the embroidery thread (floss), then add the eyes and rosy cheeks, following the instructions on page 8, see Figure C. Sew on shell buttons if desired (see photo).

C

FLORAL DOVES

YOU WILL NEED

- *Fabric for the body*
- *Contrasting fabric for the wings*
- *Volume interfacing*
- *Stuffing*
- *Fine steel wire*
- *Paint for the eyes and bill*
- *Blusher or lipstick for the cheeks*
- *Pointed wooden garden cane*

HOW TO MAKE

BODY AND WINGS

Read the section on 'Stuffed Forms' on pages 8–9 before starting.
 Fold the fabric for the body double, right sides facing. Transfer the pattern to the fabric. Cut out a piece of fabric large enough for two sets of wings and iron the volume interfacing to the reverse side of half the fabric piece. Fold double, right sides facing.

Use a thicker steel wire for mounting the dove if you decide to create a larger design.

Transfer the pattern for the wings to the fabric. Sew around the outline of the wings and body, see Figure A. Cut out, turn right side out and press the pieces. Stuff the bird and fold the opening the opposite way so that the seams are aligning. Fold in the seam allowance and insert the centre portion of a length of wire so that the ends emerge at either end of the opening. Sew up the opening, see Figure B. Then sew up the opening on the wings.

As marked on the pattern, top stitch the wings, machine stitching from the edge of the wings inwards a little, see Figure C.

A

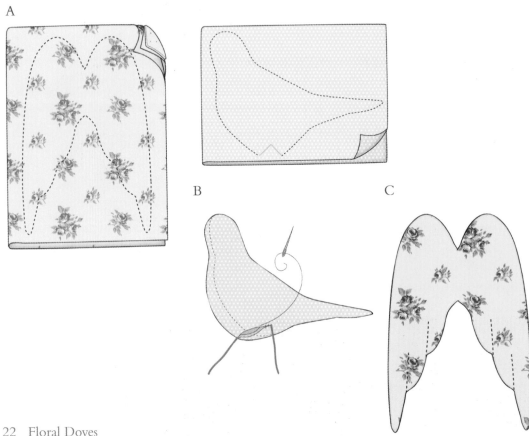

B

C

FINISHING TOUCHES

Glue or sew the wings to the bird's body – use the photos as a guide to positioning. Add the eyes and rosy cheeks, following the instructions on page 8. Cut the pointed end off the cane for the bill. Paint it in your chosen colour and glue it on the bird.

Experiment with different patterned and floral fabrics to create a beautiful assortment of colourful doves.

ROYAL HENS

HOW TO MAKE

BODY AND WINGS

Read the section on 'Stuffed Forms' on pages 8–9 before starting.

Sew together a strip of fabric for the body and a strip of patterned fabric for the pantaloons. Press the seam allowances away from each other. Fold the fabric double, right sides facing. Transfer the pattern and sew from point A to point B, as marked see Figure A.

A

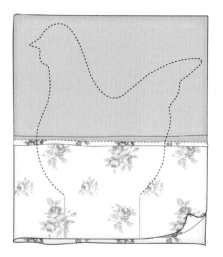

These hens can be placed in old jugs and vases to create pretty ornaments for a country kitchen.

PANTALOONS

Cut out the hen and add an extra seam allowance at the bottom along the opening. Fold the hen the opposite way so that the seams are aligning.

Sew the bottom section to create pantaloon legs, see Figure B. Sew the seam twice to make it stronger. Turn the hen right side out. Fold under the seam allowance at the bottom of each pantaloon leg and press the hen.

Stuff the body and partway down each leg. Sew running stitches around each pantaloon leg 1cm (⅜in) up from the folded edge without fastening the thread.

Paint the canes pink, then push and twist the pointed ends into the hen through the pantaloon legs. Pull the thread to gather the pantaloon legs around the legs, see Figure C and stitch in place.

Sew a length of lace around the top edge of the pantaloons.

B

C

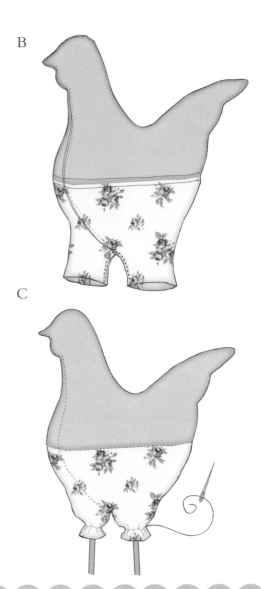

WINGS

To make the wings, fold the fabric double and transfer the pattern, flipping it to make the second wing. Make the opening for reversing through one of the fabric layers, making sure that each opening is on the opposite side for one left and one right wing.

Sew around the outlines. Cut out, snipping into the seam allowance where the seam points sharply inwards. Use a wooden stick to turn the wings right side out. Press the wings and top stitch from the edge of the wings inwards.

Stuff the channels between the top stitching with the help of the stick, then stuff the rest of the wings before you sew up the opening.

FINISHING TOUCHES

Paint the beak and the wattle pink. Add the eyes and rosy cheeks, following the instructions on page 8.

Glue the crown to the head and stitch the wings to the body. Insert the hen in a pot filled with florist's foam and arrange moss on top.

DUCK POND

YOU WILL NEED
- *Fabric for the head*
- *Fabric for the body and wings*
- *Lace or ribbon*
- *Paint for the bill and eyes; blusher or lipstick for the cheeks*
- *Stuffing*

HOW TO MAKE

HEAD AND BODY

Read the section on 'Stuffed Forms' on pages 8–9 before starting.

  Sew together a piece of fabric large enough to cut out two duck heads and a piece of fabric large enough to cut out two duck bodies.

The duckling is made in the same way as the mother duck, but using one piece of fabric and without wings.

Fold the fabric double, right sides facing, transfer
the pattern and sew around the outline, see
Figure A. Cut out.

Fold the openings at the bottom front and back
the opposite way and sew across to create a base,
see Figure B. Turn right side out and press, then
stuff and sew up the remaining opening.

A

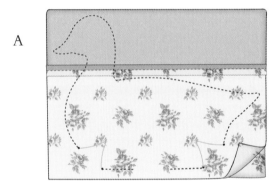

B

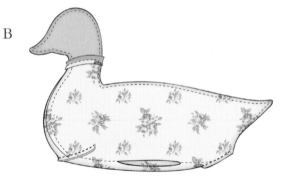

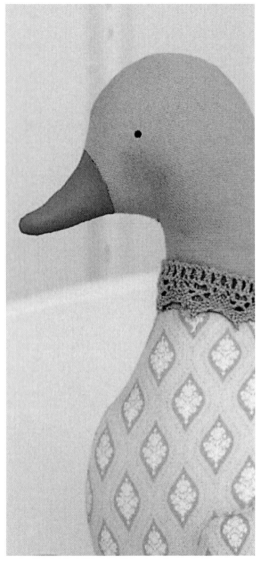

WINGS

Make the wings by folding the fabric double and transferring the pattern, flipping it to make the second wing.

Sew around the outlines. Cut out, snipping into the seam allowance where the seam points sharply inwards. Use a wooden stick to turn the wings right side out. Press the wings and top stitch from the edge of the wings inwards, see Figure C.

Stuff the channels between the top stitching with the help of the stick, then stuff the rest of the wings before you sew up the opening. Sew them on to the sides of the duck – use the photos for positioning.

FINISHING TOUCHES

Sew a piece of lace or ribbon around the neck of the duck.

Paint the bill, then add the eyes and rosy cheeks following the instructions on page 8.

C

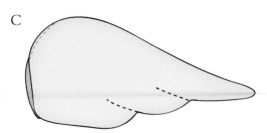

BIRD HOUSE

YOU WILL NEED

For the birds and houses:
- *Fabric for body and beak*
- *Fabric for the house*
- *Striped fabric for the roof*
- *Stuffing*
- *Button*

For the wreath:
- *Straw wreath 30cm (12in)*
- *Root threads*
- *Thin wire*
- *Scissors*
- *Glue gun*

HOW TO MAKE

Read the section on 'Stuffed Forms' on pages 8–9 before starting.

You can use the birds and houses to create either a pot decoration or a wreath (see page 35). For the pot decoration, make a small opening in the border seam on the reverse side of the house and insert a stick. Push into a plant pot filled with florist's foam and decorative straw.

The simple bird design really brightens up a little drawstring bag.

32

BIRD

Cut out the parts for the body from the pattern. Cut a square 4 × 4cm (1½ × 1½in) for the beak. Fold the fabric for the beak in two, then fold the corners down sidelong so the middle of the fabric is shaped as a tip, see Figures A and B.

Place the body parts for the bird right sides together with the beak in between, and sew around. If the back part of the bird is not going to show, you can make the reversing opening through one of the fabric layers, see Figure C. Cut away any superfluous fabric from the beak before you turn it right side out and stuff, referring to the instructions on pages 8–9.

HOUSE

Cut out a piece for the house without the roof and two pieces of roof for the front. Cut out the whole house for the back piece. Sew the roof pieces to the house piece so that the border will appear where it's marked on the pattern. Put the front and the back pieces right sides together and sew around, see Figure D.

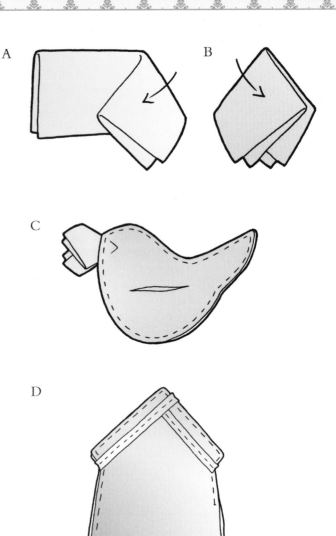

A

B

C

D

WREATH

If the bird house is being made for a wreath, sew around the border and make a cut on the back to reverse and stuff it. Turn the bird house right side out and stuff. Glue the button to the front. Make the wreath by wiring bunches of root threads around a straw wreath, see Figure E. Use a pair of scissors to style the wreath as you wish before attaching the figures with a glue gun.

E

BUSY CHICKENS

YOU WILL NEED
- *Light or dark brown linen for the body*
- *Terracotta linen for beak, comb and legs*
- *Fabric for the dungarees*
- *Stuffing*
- *Fabric paints for the face and embroidery threads for the clothes*

HOW TO MAKE

BODY

Read the section on 'Stuffed Forms' on pages 8–9 before starting.

Fold the brown linen double, right sides together, and trace the pattern for the body. Cut away enough fabric so that you can sew on two pieces of terracotta linen where the beak will be, and trace the beak.

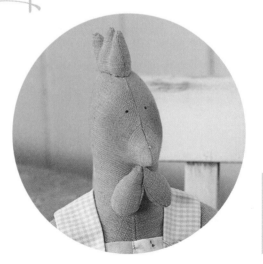

Enlarge the pattern on a photocopier to 120% to make the bigger chicken.

Sew around the body and beak, see Figure A. Cut out, and turn the body inside out. With the brown linen double, trace the pattern for the wings and sew around, see Figure B.

Fold the terracotta linen double, right sides together. Trace the patterns for the comb and wattle and sew around, see Figure C.

Cut out and turn all the parts inside out. Stuff the body and wings as described on page 9. Fold in the seam allowance around the opening on the comb, and stuff the comb and wattle using a stick to get into the corners. Sew up the wattle opening.

A
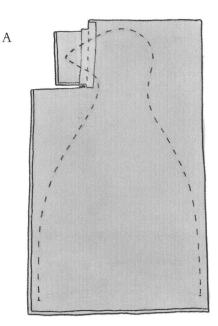

B
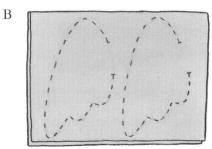

C
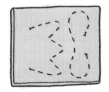

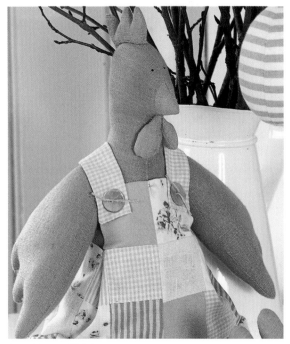

FEET

Cut a piece of terracotta linen 21 × 14cm (8½ × 5½in) for the feet. Press down 1cm (½in) at the top and bottom, see Figure D.

Place the fabric flat with the folded edges facing down, then fold up 3cm (1¼in) at the bottom and fold the top edge down so that the pressed edges meet, with the folds now facing up, see Figure E. Trace the feet so that the dotted line on the pattern matches the opening between the folds and sew around, see Figure F.

Cut out, turn inside out and stuff the feet as described on pages 8–9.

D

E

F

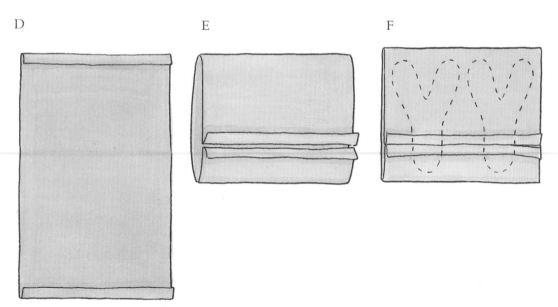

LEGS

To make the legs, fold the fabric in half and place the pattern along the fold. Cut out two and sew along the long and short edges. Turn inside out and press. Fold in the seam allowance around the opening and stuff the legs using a wooden stick. Tack the open ends of the legs on to the feet to cover the foot openings, see Figure G.

Place the other ends of the legs into the bottom of the body. Sew across the opening so that the legs are fastened. Stitch on the wings. Fold the wattle in half and stitch it under the beak. Sew the comb to the head and paint the face as described on page 8, see Figure H.

G

H

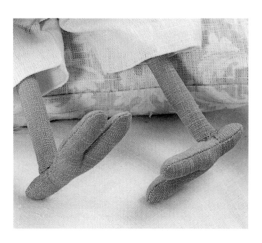

DUNGAREES

The patchwork dungarees are made from 4.5cm (2in) patches plus seam allowance.

Fold the fabric in half and place the pant pattern on the fold. Cut out two dungaree pant pieces, adding extra seam allowances at the waist and the bottom of the legs. Cut out a bib piece with extra seam allowances round three sides.

Place the two pant pieces with right sides together, and sew up one side along the curved edge, see Figure I.

Turn and press the seam allowance across the top and each side of the bib. Insert lengths of iron-on tape and iron to hold.

With right sides facing sew on the bib across the centre seam of the dungaree pants. Fold down the waist hem and press with the bib up. Embroider a heart by hand or machine over the seam, see Figure J.

I

J

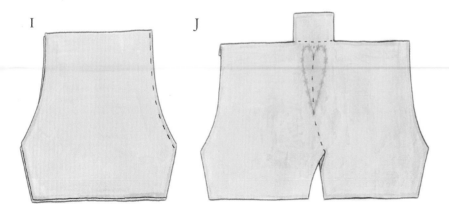

Fold the pants with right sides together and sew along the other curved edge.

Fold the dungaree pants the other way so that the seams now match each other and sew the legs, see Figure K.

Press seams open. Fold up the seam allowance at the bottom of each leg, insert iron-on tape and press to hold. Turn inside out and put the dungarees on the figure.

Make two tucks at the front, one on each side of the bib and two at the back so that the dungarees fit at the waist. Stitch the tucks to hold.

K

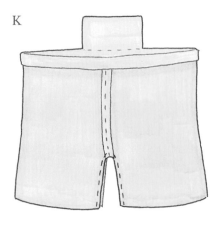

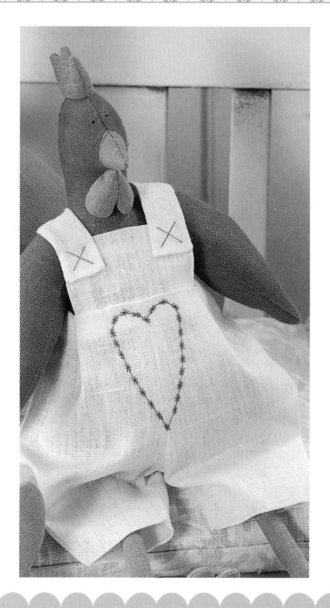

To make the straps, fold the fabric in half and place the pattern for the straps along the fold. Cut out two straps and sew along the long and one short edge, see Figures L and M. Turn the straps inside out and press.

Put the pants on the figure. Stitch two tucks at the front of the pants, one on each side of the bib, and two at the back, so that it fits the body.

Sew on the straps and fasten with crosses or buttons at the top of the bib. Cross them at the back, insert inside the waist and stitch to hold.

Fold a big tuck at the outside bottom edge of each dungaree leg and stitch to hold, see Figure N.

N

L

M

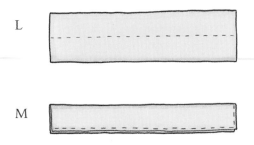

OYSTER CATCHERS

YOU WILL NEED
- *Fabric for the body*
- *Stuffing*
- *Three pointed wooden garden canes*
- *Paint for the bill and legs*

HOW TO MAKE
Sew the body and wings in the same way as for the Seaside Puffins on pages 16–19, but note that there is no opening under the bird to be folded the opposite way, just a straight opening for reversing. Simply push and twist the sharp tips of the canes through the fabric. Twist a pointed piece of cane 10cm (4in) long into the head as a bill.

The legs and bill are made using painted garden canes.

SUPPLIERS

UK
Panduro Hobby
Westway House
Transport Avenue
Brentford
Middlesex
TW8 9HF
Tel: 020 8566 1680
trade@panduro.co.uk
www.pandurohobby.co.uk

Coast and Country
Crafts & Quilts
8 Sampson Gardens
Ponsanooth, Truro
Cornwall
TR3 7RS
Tel: 01872 863894
www.coastandcountrycrafts.co.uk

Fred Aldous Ltd.
37 Lever Street
Manchester
M1 1LW
Tel: 08707 517301
www.fredaldous.co.uk

The Sewing Bee
52 Hillfoot Street
Dunoon, Argyll
PA23 7DT
Tel: 01369 706879
www.thesewingbee.co.uk

Puddlecrafts
7 St. Clair Park
Route Militaire
St. Sampson
Guernsey
GY2 4DX
Tel: 01481 245441
www.puddlecrafts.co.uk

The Fat Quarters
5 Choprell Road
Blackhall Mill
Newcastle
NE17 7TN
Tel: 01207 565728
www.thefatquarters.co.uk

Threads and Patches
48 Aylesbury Street
Fenny Stratford
Bletchley
Milton Keynes
MK2 2BU
Tel: 01908 649687
www.threadsandpatches.co.uk

USA
Coats and Clark USA
PO Box 12229
Greenville
SC29612-0229
Tel: 0800 648 1479
www.coatsandclark.com

Connecting Threads
13118 NE 4th Street
Vancouver
WA 9884
www.connectingthreads.com

eQuilter.com
5455 Spine Road, Suite E
Boulder
CO 80301
www.equilter.com

Hamels Fabrics
5843 Lickman Road
Chilliwack
British Columbia
V2R 4B5
www.hamelsfabrics.com

Keepsake Quilting
Box 1618 Center Harbor
NH 03226
www.keepsakequilting.com

The Craft Connection
21055 Front Street
PO Box 1088
Onley
VA 23418
www.craftconn.com

INDEX

accessories 7
adhesive, iron-on 7

bags, drawstring 32
Bird House 32–5
bodies
    chickens 24, 36–8
    doves 20–2
    ducks 28–30
    geese 10
    puffins 16

chickens
    Busy Chickens 36–43
    Royal Hens 24–7
clothing 13–15, 26, 41–3
    dungarees 13–14, 41–3
    hats 15
    pantaloons 26
cotton 6
crowns 27
cutting out 8

Doves, Floral 20–3
Duck Pond 28–31
ducklings 28
dungarees 13–14, 41–3

embroidery 41

fabrics 6
faces 8
    chickens 27
    doves 23
    ducks 31
    puffins 19
feet 12, 39
firm interfacing 7
fusible interfacing 7

Geese, Jolly 10–15

hats 15
heads, duck 28–30
Hens, Royal 24–7
Houses, Bird 32–5

interfacing 7
    firm 7
    fusible 7
    lightweight 7
    volume 7
iron-on adhesive 7

Jolly Geese 10–15

legs 12, 40
lightweight interfacing 7
linen 6

materials 6–7

Oyster Catchers 44–5

paints, craft 7
pantaloons 26
patterns 7
pens, vanishing ink 7
plant sticks, wooden 7
Puffins, Seaside 16–19

reversing 9
Royal Hens 24–7

scissors 7
Seaside Puffins 16–19
sewing 8
sewing machine feet,
    transparent 7
stuffed forms 8–9
stuffing
    polyester 6
    technique 9

Tilda Products 7
tools 7

volume interfacing 7

wings
    chicken 24, 27
    dove 20–2
    duck 31
    goose 10
wreaths 35

TEMPLATES

All templates need to be enlarged by 400%.
Add seam allowance for all templates, except
for the appliqué shapes.

Jolly Geese
(page 10)

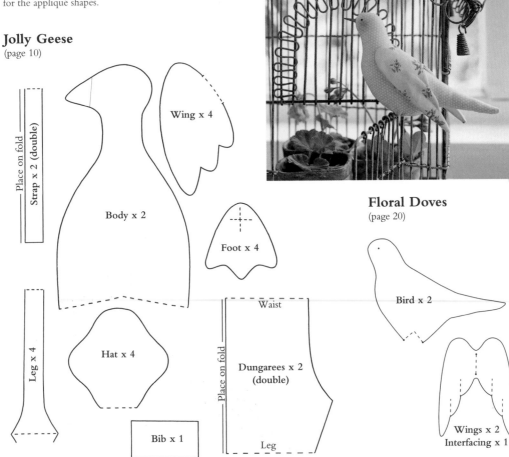

Place on fold
Strap x 2 (double)

Wing x 4

Body x 2

Foot x 4

Leg x 4

Hat x 4

Bib x 1

Waist

Place on fold

Dungarees x 2
(double)

Leg

Floral Doves
(page 20)

Bird x 2

Wings x 2
Interfacing x 1

Seaside Puffins
(page 16)

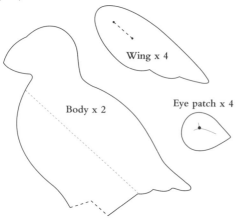

Wing x 4

Body x 2

Eye patch x 4

Royal Hens
(page 24)

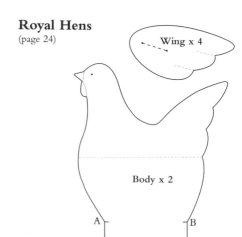

Wing x 4

Body x 2

A

B

ES

Bird House
(page 32)

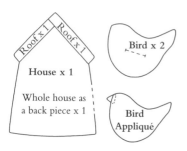

Roof x 1

Roof x 1

House x 1

Whole house as
a back piece x 1

Bird x 2

Bird
Appliqué

Busy Chickens
(page 36)

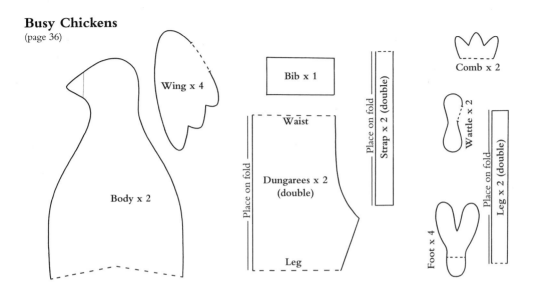

Wing x 4

Body x 2

Bib x 1

Waist

Place on fold

Dungarees x 2
(double)

Leg

Place on fold
Strap x 2 (double)

Comb x 2

Wattle x 2

Place on fold
Leg x 2 (double)

Foot x 4

Duck Pond
(page 28)

Oyster Catchers
(page 44)

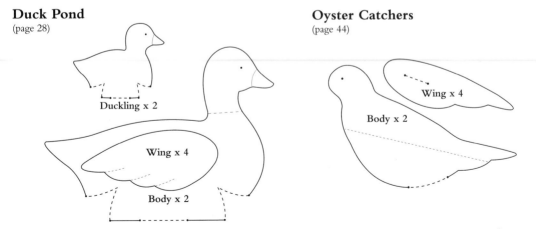

Duckling x 2

Wing x 4

Body x 2

Wing x 4

Body x 2